THE
WORD PRAYER BOOK

Winklette Mckie

Copyright © 2021 Winklette Mckie.

All rights reserved. No part of this book may be used or reproduced by any means, graphic, electronic, or mechanical, including photocopying, recording, taping or by any information storage retrieval system without the written permission of the author except in the case of brief quotations embodied in critical articles and reviews.

LifeRich Publishing is a registered trademark of The Reader's Digest Association, Inc.

LifeRich Publishing books may be ordered through booksellers or by contacting:

LifeRich Publishing
1663 Liberty Drive
Bloomington, IN 47403
www.liferichpublishing.com
844-686-9607

Because of the dynamic nature of the Internet, any web addresses or links contained in this book may have changed since publication and may no longer be valid. The views expressed in this work are solely those of the author and do not necessarily reflect the views of the publisher, and the publisher hereby disclaims any responsibility for them.

COVER IMAGE CREATED BY WINKLETTE MCKIE.

THE HOLY BIBLE, NEW INTERNATIONAL VERSION®, NIV® Copyright © 1973, 1978, 1984, 2011 by Biblical, Inc.® Used by permission. All rights reserved worldwide.

The "Amplified" trademark is registered in the United States Patent and Trademark Office by The Lockman Foundation. Use of this trademark requires the permission of The Lockman Foundation.

Scripture is taken from the New King James Version®. Copyright © 1982 by
Thomas Nelson. Used by permission. All rights reserved.

The "ESV"; and "English Standard Version" are trademarks of Good News Publishers.
Use of either trademark requires the permission of Good News Publishers.

Scripture quotations marked NLT are taken from the Holy Bible, New Living Translation, copyright © 1996, 2004, 2015 by Tyndale House Foundation. Used by permission of Tyndale House Publishers, Inc., Carol Stream, Illinois 60188. All rights reserved.

ISBN: 978-1-4897-3716-8 (sc)
ISBN: 978-1-4897-3717-5 (e)

Library of Congress Control Number: 2021914418

Print information available on the last page.

LifeRich Publishing rev. date: 07/21/2021

Acknowledgements

My most incredible honour goes to the Father, Son and Holy Spirit. Thank you to Deacon Michael Gordon, for making my university education possible. Mr Carlington Forrest, Student Affairs- University of the West Indies. My morning star Ms Whitney Richards- Norman Manly Law School.

I want to thank the many people that contributed significantly to developing my mind. Ms Rose and Ms Brown, who taught me at New Day All-Age School. Mrs Kong Fong- Foran, former Dean of Studies at St. Michael's Theological College in Jamaica. Dr Olivene Thomas and Dr Julian Devonish, who taught me at the University of the West Indies. Dr Duff, Professor Townsend, Dr C. Wilson and Dr Cho, Canada.

Introduction

Prayer is an essential tool for believers. Jesus recorded praying 25 different times in the Bible. He taught us how to pray. We can pray by kneeling, sitting, standing, with our hands lifted and face towards the ground.

It was God from the beginning, with the word, and the word was with God, and the Word was God. Who spoke, and everything took on life. We can have the same outcome when we use the written word to pray. The word of God is the authority in any form.

All spiritual warfare and deliverance prayers should only carry out by a born-again Christian who has confessed his/her sins and promised never to repeat them.

Biblical Guide For Successful Prayers

★ Don't hold on to any wilful sin.
- If you do this, then your prayer is not sincere. Isaiah 59:2 NIV Your sins have kept you from your God; your sins have concealed his face from you so that he will not receive you.

• Don't speak contrary to your prayers.
- Watch what you say. Put aside bitterness and stop cursing. James 3:10 KJV Out of the same mouth comes admiration and swearing. My brethren, this should not be.

✓ Don't be doubtful
- Exercise faith. Unbelief can cancel prayers. Matthew 17:20 AMP and Jesus said unto them, Because of your non-belief: for indeed I say unto you, if ye have faith as a grain of mustard seed, you will say unto this mountain, eradicate henceforth to yonder place, and it shall remove, and nothing shall be unbearable unto you.

★ Don't stop thanking God.
- Offer thanksgiving for your prayers that have already been answered. John 11:41 NKJV So they took away the stone. Then Jesus looked up and said, "Father, I thank you that you have heard me.

❑ Don't stop praying
- Be Steadfast. Luke 18:1 WEB Then Jesus told his disciples a parable to show them that they should always pray and not give up.

Table of Contents

Thanksgiving 1
Adoration 2
Repentance 3
Destiny 4
Shame and Reproach 5
Unjust Situation 6
Conquer Bitterness 7
Parents 8
Friendships 9
Beauty 10
Wisdom 11
Knowledge 12
Finance 13
Unemployment 14
Open Heaven 15
Grace To Submit 16
Spirit Spouses – Male & Female 17
Marital Settlement 18
Fruit of the Womb 19
Sickness 20
Remove Prion 21
PH Balance Normalize 22
Electrical & Magnetic Frequency 23
The Curse Of Dishonour 24
Grace Of Honour 25

Leadership	26
Crisis	27
Exemption	28
Criticism	29
Open Gates	30
Mercy	31
Terrorism	32
Peace Of Mind	33
Rest In Christ	34
Good Night's Sleep	35
Dominion Over Time	36
Nation	37
Invocation of Jesus's Blood	38
Draw Strength From God	39
Removing Patterns Of Curse	40
Breaking Sexual Covenants	41
Anger	42
Anxiety	43
Emotional Healing	44
Unforeseeable Future	45
Salvation Of Others	46
Breaking Limitation	47
General Self-Deliverance	48
Spiritual Warfare	49
Returning Evil Arrows	51
Prophetic Declarations	53
Surviving Seasons	55
Freedom From Spiritual Prisons	56
Forgiveness	57
Influence And Affluence	58
Facing Natural Disaster	59
Positive Thinking	60

Purging Bloodline 61
Spirit Of Control And Manipulation 62
Defeating Principalities And Powers 63
Overcome Pride And Deceit 64
Immigration Issues 65
Grace To Be Genuine 66
Dry Bones Live 67
Restitution 68
My Brothers' Keeper 69
Remembrance 70
Binding The Strong Man 71
Home Ownership 72
Calling Forth Mantles And Graces 73
Right DNA 75
Break The Curse Of Hand To Mouth 76
Abortion 77
Unnatural Desires 78
Frontline Enemy 79
Conspiracies 80
Love 81

Thanksgiving

Abba Lord, I thank You for today.

I thank You for my household and friends.

I thank You for health and strength.

I thank You for my mental clarity.

I thank You for the ability to learn.

I thank You for Your continuous provisions.

I thank You for the leaders in my country,

school, and place of worship. I thank You for the virtues carefully placed in me.

I thank You for the abilities of all men.

I thank You for world peace.

I thank You for life to make a change today.

I thank You for the death and resurrection of Jesus Christ. Abba, in the name of Your Son Jesus, I ask for my thanksgiving to be permanent and sure. Thank you, Holy Spirit.

Adoration

Vatter Lord, I humbly come before You as your son/daughter to lift You, even as You are the lifter of men.

I adore You for taking my place on the cross,

I adore You for not giving up even when You might have wanted to when You said, "My Vatter, if it is possible, let this cup taken from me. Not by my will, but if You desire it to be removed from me (Luke 22:42 KJV)."

Vatter, I adore and admire Your resistance to earthly powers and wealth.

I adore You as You sacrificed Yourself daily to work miracles in the lives of humanity.

Vatter, I lay everything I am before You; take it for Your glory. I humbly bow in mind, spirit, and body before You. Let Your inspiration flow through me to continue the work You commissioned me to do in Jesus' name. Thank you, Holy Spirit.

Repentance

Abbu-Jaan Lord, thank you for another chance to come before You to reconcile me. You are fantastic and mighty. Daily will I confess my sins to You to remain in right-standing with my heavenly Abbu-Jaan. Blessed is he whose transgressions are forgiven, whose sins covered under Jesus' blood. Blessed is the one whose sins the Lord does not count against him and in whose spirit is no deceit.

Abbu-Jaan Lord, please forgive my sins (Say what your sins are) in the name of Jesus Christ. Abbu-Jaan, just as You have forgiven me, I delight in releasing everyone who has offended me knowingly and unknowingly. Abbu-Jan, it feels great to be in good standing with you. Please extend your grace daily in Jesus' name. Thank you, Holy Spirit.

Destiny

Tatay Lord, thank You for being the Author of my life. You are the most excellent writer. Your army is mighty. Their features are that of horses; they walk along like cavalry. Their feet make thundering noises like that of chariots, and they are swift and firm. They scale over walls, like a crackling fire consuming stubble, Your mighty army set for battle (Joel 2:4 NIV).

Tatay lord, I shall run like mighty men, I desire speed to my life, just as the Lord gave forte to Elijah. He pushed his cloak into his belt and ran ahead of Ahab's chariot to the entrance of Jezreel (1 Kings 18:46 KJV).

I was born for a reason, a specific purpose.
I am not a non-entity, a biological accident.
I am not one of the many people on the earth.
I am here; it's written about me in the scroll.
I am here to fulfil Your will, my God.
I have an assignment.
I have a mandate.
I have a destiny.
I am taking back my life from the enemy
of my soul right now!
I must fulfil my purpose.

The Lord said to me, "Before you were formed in the womb, before you were born, I knew of you, I set you apart; I appointed you a bright future (Jeremiah 1:5 KJV)." My place in life, determined by You Tatay, skip the pages of the book right now in the name of Jesus Christ. Thank you, Holy Spirit.

Shame and Reproach

Atta Lord, thank You for being my all in all. You are the Lilly planted by the riverside. The morning's dew. Remove from me shame and reproach; for I have kept Your testimonies. People sat down and spoke awful things against me: but I meditate on Your statutes. My soul melted with heaviness: strengthen me according to Your word. I have renounced the hidden things of shame, not walking in craftiness, nor handling the word of God deceitfully, but by the manifestation of the truth commending myself to every man's conscience in the sight of God (2 Cor 2:4 NLT).

Atta Lord, at the right time, You will address the issue with my oppressors; You will save me and pick up the shattered pieces of my emotion, and You will turn my shame into praise, and it will be known in every land where I have suffered. I decree and declare I will have a double portion for my shame. Instead of humiliation, I will shout for joy over my breakthrough. So, I receive a double portion in the presence of those who have shamed and reproached me, everlasting joy is mine in Jesus' name. Thank you, Holy Spirit.

Unjust Situation

Baabaa Lord, I thank You for being a God who judges. Supreme, mighty You are. The One who speaks and the world formed. Vindicate me, O God, I bring into view my case against ungodly people; Please deliver me from the deceitful and unjust situation! Baabaa, thank You for, through Your words, I know that You understand what I am going through. You received unfair treatment too.

Baabaa Lord, please oppose, O Lord, those who oppose me; beatdown those who contend with me. Bring out Your sword and shield and defend me. Draw the spear and bow, bring the battle-axe to meet those who pursue me; comfort my soul, You are my deliverer.

Baabaa Lord, bring them to justice. Sorrows shall be the table set before them; may it become retribution and a trap. May their eyes darkened so they cannot see, and their backs are bent forever. Let Your wrath come upon them; let Your violent anger surpass them. May their life be deserted; let no one live in their houses. Reward injustice for injustice, don't let them enter Your righteousness without surrendering and repentance. Should they refuse to surrender and repent. Let it be that they are blotted out of the book of life, and may they not be recorded with the righteous in Jesus' name. Thank you, Holy Spirit.

Conquer Bitterness

Abbu-Jean, thank You for not holding my sins against me. You are love. The thief comes to steal, to kill, and to destroy (John 10:10 KJV). The thief is in my heart: seeking revenge. It's crying out for justice. It is motivated by the unresolved injustice which took its peace.

Abbu-Jean, I have been pleading my cause before You for justice and revenge. Without listening to the Holy Spirit which ministered to me: You are here for my captive heart. I am no longer blind. I have recovered sight, You set at liberty the bruised. I am seeking Your forgiveness and setting me free from the spirit of injustice in Jesus' name. Thank you, Holy Spirit.

Parents

Pappy Lord, thank You for giving me parents who chose to carry me. You are the great I Am. You said my parents should not treat me in such a way as to make me angry. Instead, raise me with Christian discipline and instructions. Also, that I will remember their instructions all my life. Holy Spirit, help me to respect my father and mother to have a long and fruitful life. I know their teaching will improve my character as a beautiful turban or a necklace improves my appearance; Above everything, Pappy helps us love one another earnestly because love covers many flaws in Jesus' name. Thank you, Holy Spirit.

Friendships

Apa Lord, thank You for the gift of friendship. You are Agape and Pragma together. Someone who has unreliable friends will come to ruin. Apa, guide me to choose holy and dearly loved people as my friends. Who clothes themselves with compassion, kindness, humility, gentleness, and patience? Someone who will forgive me as I will forgive them when we have a grievance against each other. A friend love never ends. Through friendship, a brother is born for adversity. Apa, help us to share brotherly love. I will forgive as the Lord forgave me. Out of all the virtues, let us put on love, which will bind us in perfect unity, in the name of Jesus Christ. Thank you, Holy Spirit.

Beauty

Abeoji Lord, thank you for the uniqueness of my body. I praise Your wonderful works. I will not worry about the changes in my body; because You will perfect everything in Your time. I declare my beauty remains like an Olive tree. I am like the strong cedar tree. I glow and blossom daily. My heart will not become proud because of my loveliness; neither will I corrupt my wisdom because of my splendour. My outward appearance represents the way I feel internally because my Abeoji has comforted me. As I become older, I will still produce fruits; I will remain vital and green. Abeoji will renew my life and sustain me as I get older. Abeoji gives long life. He will satisfy me and show me favour in Jesus' name. Thank you, Holy Spirit.

Wisdom

Baba Lord, thank you for the gift of wisdom. You are the wisest ever. I will obtain wisdom! Never will I forget her, nor turn away from the words of her mouth. I haven't forsaken her, and she has preserved me; I have loved her, and she has kept me. Wisdom is principal; so, I obtained wisdom. Endorse her, and she has promoted me; she has established me when I embraced her. A crown of grace was placed on my head; the gift of glory she will deliver to me (Proverbs 4: 5-10 NKJV).

Baba Lord, Solomon asked for wisdom, and You rewarded him. With the grace of wisdom, he ruled well, guided the people, and kept peace with other nations. For himself, he obtained wealth; no one has ever secured such wealth from his time until today. Baba, I am asking for the same proportion of wisdom You gave Solomon. I am not seeking self-gratification. If I am getting something, I want the best. With the best, I am guaranteed a better result. I will make better decisions for myself and those You entrust in my care in Jesus' name. Thank you, Holy Spirit.

Knowledge

Pater Lord, I thank You for being all-knowing. You are the most knowledgeable ever to exist. A gifted heart attains knowledge, the heart of the seeker gets understanding and the ear of the prudent seeks it out (Proverbs 18:15-16 KJV) the Lord rests on me, the spirit of Wisdom, Compassion, Counsel, Might, Knowledge and the Fear of the Lord (Isaiah 11:2 ASV). Pater, my mind has expanded; my thoughts conformed to my Pater's own.

I am excelling in all things. I can pronounce and spell all words. I am good at analyzing and resolving issues of every kind. I will continue to grow from knowledge to supernatural knowledge in the name of Jesus Christ. Thank you, Holy Spirit.

Finance

Babbo Lord, I thank You for being the owner of all things. You're the greatest financier. Who can ever be wealthier than You? The young lions lack, they suffer hunger, but You promise that I will not lack any good thing if I seek You (Psalm 34:10 NIV). Babbo, You are my provider. Your spiritual kingdom is filled with thousands of cattles on a hill; I have seen Your mighty works in the life of Jacob. You choose to bless him because Laban mistreated him. You used Your spirit cattles to mate with Laban's cattle to produce the spotted cattles Jacob saw in a vision.

Babbo Lord, just as You have singled Jacob out to bless him, please Babbo, single me out and wipe the shame from my face. You are my Shepherd, and I will never want for anything again. I call upon the God of provision in the name of Jesus Christ, my redeemer and saviour, to settle me financially. Thank you, Holy Spirit.

Unemployment

Pitar Lord, thank You for making Yourself available to me. I offer praises unto You. You're my provider, the all-sufficient One. Am not working, and in Your word, it says, "If anyone does not provide for his own, and especially his household, he has denied the faith and is worse than an unbeliever (1 Timothy 5:8 KJV)." I have limited resources to take care of my family, but I am not an unbeliever.

Pitar Lord, more than that, I rejoice in my suffering, knowing that my character will change through it. You will not allow me to be ashamed. I put all my certificates on the altar of sacrifice. Pitar, do Your will for me. Direct me to the place You want me in this season. I am leadable.

Pitar Lord, let me be a person of value in that new place. Teach me how to represent You without speaking about You. Let my hands and mind cause people to wonder, who am I in Jesus' name. Thank you, Holy Spirit, for working with me to accomplish the will of my Pitar.

Open Heaven

Daddy Lord, Thank You for being the lifter of men. When You say Yes, nobody says no. Because only You raise the poor from the dust and lift the needy from the hash heap; seat them with princes and let them inherit a throne of honour (1 Sam 2:8). Daddy, please lift me from the ash heap, and place me amongst princes and rewrite my destiny in You. For the foundations of the earth belongs to You. Oh! Daddy set me on them in the name of Jesus Christ.

B

Daddy Lord, blotting out the handwriting of ordinances speaking against me, which was contrary to me, You have blotted them out by nailing them to the cross (Col 2:14 NKJV). Daddy, blot out all that has been legally and illegally held and written against my present and future that is negative by Your might and power. When you gave Your life, You took the plans of my enemies to the cross. I present to You my current and any future ambitions as a sacrifice.

Daddy Lord, I am not blameless. Please forgive my trespasses. I rewrite my life now in the name of Jesus Christ. I declare I am spiritually healthy, walking in financial abundance; I am walking in God's purpose. My life is a testimony to all in Jesus' name. Thank you, Holy Spirit.

Grace To Submit

Father Lord, thank You for the office of marriage and a husband who fears You. The Lord is faithful to all His promises and loving towards all He has made.

Father Lord, please give me an understanding heart towards my husband. Your word says, "wife submit to your husband, as to the Lord (Ephesians 5:22 NIV)." Help me to overlook his humanity and see a man of courage.

Father Lord, help me to be humble but firm. Please help me to resist unbiblical governance tactfully; so, he will not feel small in my sight. Let me not use any member of my body to destroy my home but to build it up. In the name of Jesus Christ. Thank you, Holy Spirit.

Spirit Spouses – Male & Female

Misser Lord, thank You for letting me know through Your words that spirits can marry and create a family with me. My redeemer and friend. When men started to increase on the earth and daughters were born unto them, the children of God saw the offspring of men that they were beautiful, and they made them mates (Gen 6:2 NLT).

Misser Lord, no stranger shall continue to oppress me sexually. The door was open for them to enter. I renounce every spouse who comes through my bloodline, fornication, adultery, masturbation, or pornography. I reject you and all sexual pleasures you brought to me. The door is now closed.

I will have sex with my husband/wife and enjoy him/her. I won't have to think about someone else to be satisfied. We will obtain sexual fulfilment through each other in the name of Jesus Christ. Thank you, Holy Spirit, for leading this process.

Marital Settlement

Male

Pupa Lord, thank You for recognizing that two is better than one. Cupid You are. When a wife is found it's a decent thing. When I marry a woman, You Pupa, my creator will wed me; as a newlywed celebrates over his bride, so will You, my God, celebrate me. I place You, Lord, above every desire I have to find a wife. Please teach me how to be a husband, pupa, and priest. Let me govern my household as You would like me to, by protecting, providing, and teaching them Your ways. Thank you, Holy Spirit.

Female

Papi Lord, thank You for recognizing that two is better than one. Greatest cupid You are. Two are more valuable than one because we will have a better reward for our labour. When we fall, one is there to boost the other. But being single and fall no one is there to lift me up! Please make my heart pure, I am putting You above my desire to be found worthy as a wife. By wisdom, a house built, and through understanding, it is established; through knowledge, its rooms are filled with rare and beautiful treasures (Proverbs 24:3-4NIV). Papi, if I don't have the proper qualities to be an excellent wife, mother, and priestess, please help me to grow.

Papi lord, love is patient, kind and not proud. It does not dishonour others. It is not self-seeking. It always protects. True love never fails. Vashti is an example of a dishonouring wife. Please grant me the grace to honour like Esther and Ruth, to obtain my Boaz/Husband. Please teach me how to be a good woman in Jesus' name. Thank you, Holy Spirit.

Fruit of the Womb

Daidi Lord, thank You for making children Your priority. You are awesome! I have kept Your precepts. I am a married woman, and everyone, including myself, expects me to bear my husband's children. Children are Your gift to us. Having the fruit of the womb is my reward. Like arrows in the hand of a warrior, so are the children of one's youth. Happy is the man who has his house full of children; He shall not be ashamed but shall speak with his enemies in the gate (Psalm 127:4-5 NIV). Please, Daidi, give us what should be ours, children.

Daidi Lord, there are many women in the Bible that You favoured and gave them the fruit of the womb for different reasons. Give me children, and I will ensure that they are taught Your precepts and serve You in the best way possible in Jesus' name. Thank you, Holy Spirit, for ministering to me.

Sickness

Otosan Lord, thank You for bearing all things. You're the greatest healer. You knew me, even before my parents met. You formed every fibre of my being. You are the potter, am the clay. Your desire for me is to prosper and be in good health. You endured much whipping just for my healing.

Otosan, You are the Lord that heals. Your words have power, they healed my disease. You are my healer. You were wounded for my transgressions. You were bruised for my iniquities; the chastisement of my peace was upon Him, and with His stripes am healed (Isa 53:5 KJV). No stranger shall remain in this body. Therefore, you spirit of infirmity, I command you in the name of Jesus to leave my body. For it is written at the mention of the name of Jesus every knee must bow (Phil 2:10 ASV), so you spirit of infirmity, stranger, viper bow to the name of Jesus. I decree and declare healed in the name above all others, which is Jesus Christ.

B

Remove Prion

I command all prions to dissolve and remove from my body altogether, in the name of Jesus Christ. I command healing to every cell affected by these prions.

C

PH Balance Normalize

I command the ph. balance of this body to normalize. I command healing to every cell affected by any abnormal ph. levels, in Jesus' name.

D

Electrical & Magnetic Frequency

I command all electrical and magnetic frequencies in my body to return to normal and balance in the name of Jesus. Thank you, Holy Spirit.

The Curse Of Dishonour

Dada Lord, thank You for not being a respecter of men. I praise You for You are worthy to be praised. Honour all people. Love the brotherhood. Fear God. Honour the king (1 Peter 2:17 KJV).

Dada Lord, I don't honour all men. I look down on people for no reason or because of their disparity in life. I often respect only the office of an individual but not the person. I confess I have the spirit of pride and jealousy.

Dada Lord, You suffered no man to do Your servants wrong: You scolded royals for their sakes, saying, "Smear not my anointed, and do my prophets no harm (Psalm 105:15 KJV)." You were very angry with Aaron and Miriam for speaking against Moses; Which led to Miriam leprosy.

Please Dada, forgive me for dishonouring Your people. I can see the result of this in my life. Crippling effects spiritually and physically. I promise to honour all men. Never to look down on anyone You have chosen and anointed in Jesus' name. Thank you, Holy Spirit, for working with me to resolve the spirit of pride and jealousy.

Grace Of Honour

Apu Lord, thank You for considering humankind. You are precious. Indeed, You bless the righteous; You surround them with Your favour as with a shield. In You, I am chosen, having been predestined according to your plan—He who works out everything in stages to the purpose of His will (Romans 8:28 AMP). Let the favour of the Lord my God be upon me, and establish the work of my hands; Yes, let the results of my hands' show!

Apu Lord, my God, You are my sun and armour; the Lord grants support and honour; no decent thing does He withhold from those whose walk is faultless (Psalm 84:11 ASV). When the King's order and edict had been broadcast, young ladies were brought to the castle of Susa and placed in the devotion of Hegai. Esther was brought to the King's citadel and entrusted to Hegai, who had charge of the harem. She pleased him and got his support. Instantly he provided her with her beauty treatments and exceptional food. He assigned her seven female assistants selected from the King's palace and moved her and her helpers into the harem's best place (Esther 2:8-9).

Apu Lord, unless I receive the grace of honour, I will never self-actualize. I will always be a lamb to the slaughter. I humbly ask for the grace of honour. Let everyone who sees me love and favour me. I need grace to move from multiple years to one. Let my helpers find and honour me in the name of Jesus Christ. Thank you, Holy Spirit.

Leadership

Peder Lord, thank You for Your divine leadership in the life of my family. The leader above all leaders. How great You are. Peder, I want to represent You well in all things. I want to make good decisions and account for them—direct ambiguity and break down barriers to change.

Peder Lord, help me to be humble, never to look down on others. Empower me with Your grace to put others well-being before my own. A fool empties the soul: but a wise man keeps it in till afterwards (Proverbs 29:11 NIV). Guard my mouth, oh Lord. When I become too big, bring me down, so I will never hurt Your people. Where there is no vision, the people perish: but he that keep the law, happy is he (Proverbs 29:18 ASV). It will be in Jesus' name. Thank you, Holy Spirit.

Crisis

Tevs Lord, thank You for being the God of peace. You are wonderful! You are my strength. My heart is sorrowful, and in anguish before You, I look around, and darkness surrounds me. Have mercy on me, God, show empathy! I am looking to You for protection. I will take refuge beneath the shadow of Your wings until this violent storm passes (Psalm 57:1 NIV).

Tevs Lord, when the righteous cry for help, You hear and deliver them out of all their troubles. The Lord is close to the broken-hearted and saves the crushed in spirit (Psalm 34:18 NIV). The righteous endure many afflictions, but the Lord rescues him out of them all. He keeps all his bones, none of them broken (Psalm 34:17-8 NKJV). I boldly declare my bones will not break. There is light amid this darkness, in Jesus' name. Thank you, Holy Spirit.

Exemption

Thank you for being there when I am in trouble. Great are You, Tad. Tad Lord, You are the only one I can call on, and You honour me, just as You did for the Israelites in Goshen when they were instructed to place the blood on their doors. The first case of exemption.

Tad Lord, I am in trouble. Your child, which exempts me, I have the right to declare Your goodness in my life. To decree and claim anything within Your will for me, and it shall be done. I have the right to call forth blessings and receive these blessings.

Tad Lord, You said "to arise and shine the light has come, (Isaiah 60:1 NIV)" by Your words, I decree and declare that I will arise and shine right now! I am no longer a victim of the powers of darkness operating to hold me captive.

Tad Lord, where others must work hard and save, I will receive freely. It will never be by work shall I prosper or gain possessions. Neither will my arm bring me victory, but by the mystery of exemption operating in my life.

Tad Lord, I will no longer cry their cry; I will no longer feel their pains because of the gift of exemption. Am exempted from poverty, sickness, and failure. Indeed, they will gather, but by that mystery, Tad, You will scatter them in seven directions in Jesus' name. Thank you, Holy Spirit.

Criticism

Buwa Lord, thank you for working with me to correct my flaws. Buwa, You see the good in us praise be thy name forever. I know how You feel about me. You desire only the best for me, thoughts to give me a great end. My beloved brother/sister's heart towards me is not good; they are quick to hear, quick to speak, quick to be filled with anger towards me. My conscience is clear, but that isn't what matters. It's the Lord himself that will examine me to decide a course of action.

Buwa Lord, the righteousness of Jesus is in me. I will stay calm when insulted. An authentic witness tells the truth; a false witness tells lies. Some people make cutting remarks, but the words of the wise bring healing (Proverbs 12:17-18 NLT).

Buwa Lord, thank You for Your words of wisdom. You told me not to be quarrelsome but kind to everyone, able to teach, patiently enduring evil, and correcting my opponents with gentleness (2 Timothy 2:24-26 NLT). Buwa! Please extend repentance to them, leading to a knowledge of the truth. Quench the terrorizing tongue of men. Please help me to remain steadfast and secure in the name of Jesus Christ. Thank you, Holy Spirit.

Open Gates

Opa Lord, You are in control of all systems, thank You. You are the most significant inventor. Mighty gates open. Let the gates open wide, by divine authority O gates, open! Just as you did for Peter and the Angel. They passed the first and second guard, then reached the iron gate that leads into the city. It unlocked for them by itself, and they exit; so, shall the iron gate be open for me to go out from a place of stagnancy.

Opa Lord, let the gate of influence, business, ministries, wealth, health, happiness, compassion, good leadership characteristics, peace, forerunner, humility, marriage, childbearing, family support, good friendships and education open to me now. I decree and declare my gates will be open continually. They will not be closed day or night so that men may bring me their nations' wealth, with their head of state-lead the procession in Jesus' name. Thank you, Holy Spirit.

Mercy

Father Lord, thank You for having a seat just for mercy pleas. You are most considerate. A God of mercy. My life is not moving forward; I have done everything in my strength, and I haven't changed my life circumstances.

Father Lord, I require Your mercy. It was Your mercy that caused Moses to grow up and eat in the house of Pharoah, the man who sought to kill him. Please grant me the gift of mercy.

Father Lord, I am giving You everything: my intellect, personality, passion, beauty, and pains. Please listen to me and answer me. I am poor and helpless. Protect me because I worship You only. My God, save me, Your Son/daughter who trusts in You.

Father Lord, have mercy upon me because I have called on You all day (Psalm 86:3 NIV). Give happiness to me, Your child, because I dedicate my life to You ultimately, lord. Father Lord, You are kind and forgiving and have a great love for those who call unto You. Father Lord, hear my prayer and please listen when I ask for mercy. I call upon You in times of trouble because I know You will hear and answer me.

Father Lord, there is no other like You and no works like Yours. Father Lord, You are great, and You perform miracles. Only You are God. Father Lord, teach me Your ways, and I will live by Your truth. Please give me the grace to respect You completely, the God of mercy in the name of Jesus Christ. Thank you, Holy Spirit.

Terrorism

Far Lord, thank You for Your promises to keep us safe. My strong arm and a tower of strength. Hear my voice, O God, in my complaint; Preserve the life of my nations' people from the dread of the enemy. There are secret counsels of people with hidden agendas. I know You will pull us out of the net they have secretly laid. You are our strength.

Far Lord, who brings us out from our enemies? Even lift us above those who rise against us; You will rescue us from the violent man. Keep us, O Lord, from the hands of the wicked; Preserve us from violent men (Psalm 18:48 NKJV) whose intent to destroy this country?

Far Lord, You will keep our soul. Arise, O Lord, in Your anger; rise against the rage of our enemies: principalities, powers, rulers of darkness; spiritual wickedness in high places, make a show of them openly. Awake, my God, decree justice. O righteous God brings an end to the violence of the wicked and makes the righteous secure (Psalm 7:6-11NIV). They formed together against the righteous and convicted the blameless to death. But the Lord has been our grip, rock of protection. He will put upon them their evil and terminate them for their wickedness. The Lord, our God, will dismantle them and restore peace in Jesus' name. Thank you, Holy Spirit.

Peace Of Mind

Bap Lord, I thank You for calming raging waters. You are my peace. In this world, I will have trouble. But I know the heart You have towards me; Your wish is that I will be stable- because You have resisted the world's gifts. I obtain peace because the Lord of peace has always given me peace. The peace of Christ shall rule in my life. I shall always be thankful. You have left Your peace with me; Your vocation You have given me. You do not deliver to me as the world does. Bap, I will not let my heart be troubled and be afraid (John 14:1 ASV). I take comfort in Your words.

Bap Lord, You strengthen me; You bless me with peace. With You, I don't have to be anxious about anything. In every situation, by prayer and supplication, I present my requests to You with thanksgiving (Phil 4:6 NKJV). And the peace of Bap, which transcends all understanding, will guard my heart and my mind in Jesus' name. Thank you, Holy Spirit.

Rest In Christ

Ayah Lord, thank You that when my burdens are too much, I can lean on You. My strong tower and source of strength. Create in me a clean heart, O God, and renew a right spirit within me. Cast me not away from Your presence or take Your Holy Spirit from me. Restore to me the joy of Your salvation and grant me a spirit to sustain me (Psalm 51:10-12 KJV).

Ayah Lord, I will not lose heart. Though outwardly, I am wasting away, yet inwardly I'm renewed day by day. I embrace Your yoke upon me and learn from it, for Your gentle and humble in heart, I will find rest for my soul (Matt 11:28-30 NKJV).

Ayah Lord, my trust is steadfast in You. I don't have to be weary at all, for You, oh Lord, invited me to come unto You if I am burden and heavy laden, and You will give me rest (Matt 11:28 NIV). Please return to your rest, O my soul for Christ Jesus has dealt bountifully with you in Jesus' name. Thank you, Holy Spirit.

Good Night's Sleep

Abbu-Ji Lord, You separated night from day just for sleep, thank You. You are my four-poster bed with a platform base, mattress, pillows, and mosquito mesh surrounding it. I praise You. When I lie down, I will not be afraid (Proverbs 3:24 NLT). When I lie down, my sleep will be sweet. Your peace You leave with me, Your peace You give unto me. You do not give to me as the world gives. I will not let my heart be troubled and will not be afraid (John 14:27 NLT). For You have not given me an essence of fear, but a spirit of love, and power, and a sound mind (2 Timothy 1:7 NIV).

Abbu-Ji, I live each day to glorify Your name. For You, Lord gives to Your beloved sleep. I put my trust in You. When I lie down and sleep, it shall be in peace, (Matt 11:28 NIV) for You alone, O Lord, make me dwell in safety. I will not be afraid of the terror that takes place at night (Psalm 91:5 NIV). Abbu-Ji will give His angels charge over me (Psalm 91:11 NKJV). I will not be anxious about anything but present my requests to God with thanksgiving in every situation by prayer and petition (Philippians 4:6-7 NIV). The peace of God that exceeds all wisdom will guard my heart and my mind in Jesus' name. Thank you, Holy Spirit.

Dominion Over Time

Faoir, You are Lord over all things, thank You. You are the highest authority, and everything must bow to You. I don't know the heavens' ordinances or fix their rule over the earth (Job 38:33 NASB). Onto You, O Lord is greatness, power, glory, victory, and majesty. Surely, everything in the heavens and the earth; Yours is their dominion, O Lord, and You exalt Yourself as head overall (1 Chronicles 29:11 NASB).

Faoir Lord, there is a period and a time for every purpose to be fulfilled. Lord, it's my time to move like a Tornado. Crushing and overtaking everything in my way. I have lost years. I must recover the years that the locust, cankerworm, caterpillar, and the palmerworm, hath eaten (Joel 2:25 NIV). A great army You will send to fight with me.

Faoir Lord, on the day You gave the Amorites over to Israel, Joshua said to You in the presence of Israel: O sun, stand still over Gibeon, O moon, over the Valley of Aijalon (Joshua 10:12 NIV). So, the sun was still, and the moon stopped, till the nation avenged itself on its enemies. The sun and the moon represent time. I call on the God who is the master of time, to cease it, right now on my behalf.

Faoir Lord, now that time is standing still, I will move like a Tornado and overtake (say everything you want to recover in fullness) in the name of Jesus. Thank you, Holy Spirit.

Nation

Pere Lord, You single out men to form nations; thank You for foreseeing the need. The God who sees. You promise that violence shall no longer be heard in my land, neither wasting nor destruction within my borders, but I shall call my walls salvation and my gates Praise (Isaiah 60:18 KJV).

Pere Lord (say the name of your country) will experience a complete change in the economic and lawbreaking atmosphere. I will no longer hear that the innocent has lost their life. The tugs have changed; salvation surrounds them like a wall. Praises on their lips. They speak aloud for all to know they have changed.

Pere Lord, I pray for the heads of state in my nation (say the name of your country) to understand something clearly at last, that their rule was appointed by You. I make supplications and give thanks to You for the people and leaders of (say the name of your country). Let the leaders be upright and rule by the fear of the Lord. Let all my leaders bow down before You, Lord.

Pere Lord, my nation will serve Jesus, let all idolaters, obeah workers, sorcerers, witches, wizards, marine and forest spirits be confounded and brought to disgrace. Save (say the name of your country) and send prosperity. I pray Jesus will be (say the name of your country) heart.

Pere Lord, let all hidden treasures surface and be beneficial to the people. Revive all rivers and streams. Let the land yield as if rested for 14 years. Let the land provisions be enormous, rich in colour and nutrients.

Pere Lord, I call forth gold, oil, natural gases, diamond, precious stones to be located in my country, in Jesus' name. Thank you, Holy Spirit.

Invocation of Jesus's Blood

El Papacito Lord, thank You for allowing Your only Son to die for humanity. You're selfless. You reconcile to Yourself all things, whether things on earth or things in heaven, by making peace through Your blood, which You offered on the cross (Colossians 1:20 NIV). I invoke the blood of Jesus Christ to speak on my behalf. I decree and declare, every yoke, every spell and every ordinance speaking against my loved ones and me was appropriated with His blood on the cross. El Papacitos' blood is speaking on our behalf. I decree and declare that everything the devil has taken away from my family must return in the name of Jesus. I decree and declare that every system that spoke against my father and mother must silence through the blood of Jesus. Spirit behind every tragedy, failures, delays, lack of progression, every illegal justice system must bow to the blood of Jesus Christ in Jesus name. Thank you, Holy Spirit.

Draw Strength From God

Pabbi Lord, You are a tower of strength, thank You. Mighty One. I am in the wilderness; my life is arid. Sustain me where I am and lead me, oh Pabbi. Please respond. Your words to me are You have loved me with an everlasting love (Jeremiah 31:3 KJV). You confirmed Your love towards me, in that, while I was a sinner, Pabbi You died for me. Give unto me, according to the riches of Your glory strength to my inner being (Ephesians 3:16 ESV). I draw strength from Your love. The most excellent demonstration of Your love towards me is by giving Your only begotten Son to die for my sins.

Pabbi Lord, I know You don't want me to grieve, for Your joy is my forte. I will not be in anguish, for You are with me; I will not be discouraged, for You are my Pabbi. You will support and help me; You will sustain me with Your righteousness. You are my strength and my song; You have given me victory. Pabbi, Your words build me; it works as a therapeutic aid. I am transformed and strengthened in the name of Jesus Christ. Thank you, Holy Spirit.

Removing Patterns Of Curse

Otec Lord, I am thankful that when Jesus went to the cross, He took curses and nailed them there. Jesus, You're my perfect sacrifice. You desire that I confess my sins and the sins of my fathers, and You will heal us. Otec, I take responsibility for my sins. I ask for Your forgiveness. Separate me from my sins and the sins of my fathers. When You went to the cross, it was for our sake, for the total redemption of our transgression. Otec Lord now breaks every pattern of curse from our lives forever in the name above all names, which is Jesus Christ. Thank you, Holy Spirit.

Breaking Sexual Covenants

Patri, I thank You for being Lord over all covenants. You are special. I understand that sexual intercourse is a sign of a marriage covenant, and You refer to marriage as holy. You state that sex that takes place outside marriage is a sin. I also understand that everyone I have sex with we have entered a marriage covenant.

Patri Lord, I renounce every ungodly soul tie I have formed with (Say the name(s) of those you had sex with). It is a sin, and I renounce it as such. Separate this sin from me and my household in the name of Jesus Christ.

Patri Lord, I declare my body is the Holy Spirit's special domain, and I will no longer defile it. I will wait on the husband /wife-You have for me by Your grace and mercy in Jesus' name. Thank you, Holy Spirit.

Anger

Ojciec Lord, You are the maker of my emotions, thank You. Praise be to God everything subjected to You Ojciec. My heart is pounding, my chest is uncomfortable, and I am feeling irritated. You told me in times like this, I must put aside anger and apply good sense, which will make me slow to anger, and it is to Your glory to overlook an offence (Proverbs 19:11 ESV). Anger is a normal emotion. It is only a problem when it causes me to sin.

Ojciec Lord, my anger is out of control. Please help me not let the sun go down on my anger, where it will turn into rage and give way to the devil. Whoever is slow to anger is better than the mighty, and he who rules his spirit more than he who takes a city (Proverbs 16:32 KJV). I call upon the God of counsel to help me work through this anger issue in the name of Jesus Christ. Thank you, Holy Spirit.

Anxiety

Edesapa Lord, I thank and praise You because You have already spoken on this matter. You don't want me to be anxious over anything, but in everything, by prayer and supplication with thanksgiving, let my requests be known to You. The peace of God, which surpasses every wisdom, will guard my heart and mind (Philippians 4:6-7 NKJV) in Christ Jesus.

Edesapa Lord, I am restless, worried, trembling and feeling a sense of impending danger. One of human most common mental disorders is Anxiety. As Your son/daughter, I don't need to remain like this. Edesapa, You got this! Your shoulders are big enough to carry anything stress I am enduring. Most things I worry about I cannot change anyway, so I choose to leave them in the hands of the One who can do everything.

Edesapa Lord, by Your grace, I will not worry about tomorrow, for tomorrow will worry about itself. Each day has enough trouble of its own (Matthew 6:34 NIV). I call upon the God of peace to restore my mind in the name of Jesus Christ. Thank you, Holy Spirit.

Emotional Healing

Missier Lord, I thank You for being concerned with everything that concerns me. You are my keeper. I am in a state of turmoil. I am trusting Your words to bring forth reason and calmness to my emotion. By the Lord's strength, I will walk by the spirit and try not to gratify my flesh's desires. For the flesh's desires are against the spirit, and the spirit's wishes are against the flesh (Galatians 5:17 NLT), for they opposed each other to keep me from obtaining stability.

Missier Lord, when my emotions are stable, love, joy, peace, patience, kindness, goodness, faithfulness, gentleness, self-control be seen in me. Lord, help me and show mercy. With Christ who strengthens me-I will accomplish everything.

Missier Lord, I will make every effort to supplement my faith by employing virtue, virtue through knowledge, knowledge by self-control, self-control with steadfastness, steadfastness with godliness, and godliness through brotherly affection, and brotherly affection with love. For if these qualities are mine and are increasing, they keep me from being useless or unproductive in the familiarity of our Lord Jesus Christ (2 Peter 1:5-8 ESV). Cleansed from my former sins in Jesus' name. Thank you, Holy Spirit.

Unforeseeable Future

Aita Lord, You are gracious and perfect in all Your ways, thank You. You are the One who sees all things. Extending praises to You. The One who causes things to be. I am afraid of the future. I am unable to foresee my life. I am concerned about my future. Will things continue to be the same?

Aita Lord, You promise that You will never leave nor forsake me. I will not be afraid or discouraged. Aita has my best interest at heart. All things work for the good of those who love him, who are called according to Your purpose (Romans 8:28 ESV).

Aita Lord, I will not fear, for I am redeemed; You have called me by name; I am Yours. Unwavering love casts out all fear. Aita, You are my rock, my fortress and my deliverer. I call upon the God of courage to be with me in the name of Jesus Christ. Thank you, Holy Spirit.

Salvation Of Others

Pai Lord, thank You for making salvation accessible. You are self-giving. God so loved the world, and he gave his only begotten Son that whosoever believes in him will not perish but have everlasting life (John 3:16 AMP). Lord (call the name of the person you are praying for) believes in you but has not made a personal decision to make You Lord. Please offer to him/her the gift of salvation because unless You call him/her, he/she cannot receive the gift of salvation. Thank you, Holy Spirit, for ministering to (say his/her name) right now as I speak to Jesus on his/her behalf in Jesus' name. Thank you, Holy Spirit.

B

Pai Lord, You're not slow to fulfil Your promises, as some count slowness, but are patient, not wishing any should perish, but that all should reach repentance and obtain everlasting life through the gift of salvation (2 Peter 3:9 WEB). I, at this moment, ask for mercy and grace for (call the name of the person you are praying for) he/she does not accept that You're lord. Please cause a life-changing event to happen where he/she realizes that You are sincere, and their rescuing could only have been You in Jesus name. Thank you, Holy Spirit, for the change in his/her mindset.

Breaking Limitation

Papa, thank You for being my deliverer. Magnificent in all Your ways. Papa Lord shall liberate even the lawful captives. You came that I may have life and have it to the fullest. The word of God said, if I decree and declare a thing, it receives life. I stay to the false representative of Destiny and Nature, give up your stronghold over my life in the name of Jesus Christ.

Papa Lord, You are the real big man over Destinies and Nature. Please reveal what I must do to have a breakthrough, to end poverty and lack in my life. I will achieve my potential, talent, or gift to catapult me to greatness in the physical realm. Know that God, the creator of the universe, has no limit. I know that God's power is so much more remarkable than all others. Nothing is impossible for Him to do regarding the limitations that are challenging my existence in life. Therefore, I declare them over in Jesus' name. Thank you, Holy Spirit.

General Self-Deliverance

Pop Lord, thank You, Lord, for the process of deliverance. You command us to cast out spirits—master overall being. Everything must bow to You, Pop. For we fight not against flesh and blood, but principalities, powers, rulers of the darkness of this creation, and spiritual wickedness in high places (Ephesians 6:12 NIV).

Pop Lord, I have broken the border of protection in my life by committing the sins of (say the sins you have committed). Lord, I have confessed my sins and promised by Your grace not to repeat these sins. Please, Pop, forgive me and allow the Holy Spirit to throw out the once legal occupant(s) and take his place.

I submit to You, Pop Lord. Spirit of darkness, turmoil, and instability leave my life now in the name of Jesus Christ. Go back to the dry places. I adorn myself with the whole armour of God to close every door to possession in Jesus' name. Thank you, Holy Spirit.

Spiritual Warfare

Ama Lord, thank You for keeping my mind, body, and spirit. I offer praises to You because there's no other who is worthy of being praised. You are a great God, strong and victorious Lord.

Ama Lord, You know I am not wrestling against flesh and blood, but principalities, powers and rulers of this dark world (Ephesians 6:12 NIV). Therefore, I put on the whole garment of God, and am fully prepared for battle. I pray these words are guided by You so that I don't pray amiss.

The weapons of my warfare are not carnal but mighty to the pulling down of strongholds (2 Corinthians 10:4 NKJV). The Lord is my light and my redemption; whom shall I fear (Psalm 27:1 ESV). I stand upon the authority and strength of the Lord Jesus Christ in battle; because he is my battle axe and weapons of war (Jeremiah 51:20 KJV).

I will not fear them, for the Lord, my God is the one fighting for me. Ama, You are my war club, my weapon for battle, with You I shatter nations, with You I destroy kingdoms (Jeremiah 51:20 NIV).

Praise be to the Lord my tower of strength, who trains my hands for war, my fingers for battle. He is my loving God and my fortress, my stronghold and my deliverer, my shield, in whom I take refuge, who subdues people under me (Psalm 144:1-2 NIV).

The Lord caused my enemies to rise against me only to defeat them before me. When they come against me one way, they shall flee before me seven ways (Deuteronomy 28:7 ESV). The Lord, my God, is a consuming fire. He goes before me to destroy my enemies and make the crooked places straight in my life.

The Lord my breaker, He will break in pieces the gates of bronze and cut iron bars (Isaiah 45:2 NIV). As the Lord indicated, He the Lord my God shall destroy them quickly (Deuteronomy 9:3 KJV). Can you take loot from warriors or captives rescued from the fierce? Yes, prisoners of war will be taken from warriors and plunder retrieved from the fierce; He will contend with those who oppose my children and me; he will save us. He will make our oppressors eat their flesh; they will be drunk on their blood, as with wine. Then all humanity will know that He, the Lord, is my saviour, my redeemer, the Mighty One of Jacob (Isaiah 49:26 NIV) in Jesus' name. Thank you, Holy Spirit, for carrying out the works of God in my life.

Returning Evil Arrows

Tata Lord, I thank You for redeeming qualities. Thank You for Your sacrifice on the cross. I am thanking You for loving me unconditionally even when I don't deserve to be loved. Mighty warrior.

Tata Lord, my sins are forever before me; I am a sinner and in need of Your mercy and forgiveness. Lord, please extend forgiveness to me and help me to have peace within.

Tata Lord, I place You above all things because You are worthy to be always lifted. You are the most significant artist ever; Michael Angelo, Whitney Richards, Clever and others with artistic abilities cannot measure up to Yours, Lord. You are beautiful; You are a darling, You're mighty, You are a strong tower, a shelter, financier, an engineer, horticulturist, teacher, friend, most of all, You are my Tata and Lord.

I stand boldly on the authority given to me when I accepted Jesus Christ as Lord and Saviour of my life. Life of humankind is in the blood, and he has substituted His blood with mine to make atonement on the altar (Leviticus 17:11 WEB); it is the blood of Jesus that will speak and seek vengeance right now.

With the power and blood of Jesus Christ, I remove all arrows of delay.

With the power and blood of Jesus Christ, I remove all arrows of aborted dreams.

With the power and blood of Jesus Christ, I remove all arrows of sorrows.

With the power and blood of Jesus Christ, I remove all arrows of poverty.

With the power and blood of Jesus Christ, I remove all arrows of bloodline impurity.

With the power and blood of Jesus Christ, I remove all arrows of sickness.

With the power and blood of Jesus Christ, I remove all arrows of self-inflicted pain.

With the power and blood of Jesus Christ, I remove all arrows of depression.

With the power and blood of Jesus Christ, I remove all arrows of wayward thinking.

With the power and blood of Jesus Christ, I remove all arrows of immoral desires.

With the power and blood of Jesus Christ, I remove all arrows of low self-esteem.

With the power and blood of Jesus Christ, I remove all arrows of anger.

With the power and blood of Jesus Christ, I remove all arrows of family disunity.

I removed all the arrows in my life. I now cleansed the infected areas with the blood of Jesus Christ. My wounds have healed; Now I stand on the strength of He who is more potent than all other powers and return every arrow to their sender in the highest name Jesus Christ. Holy Spirit, thank you for carrying out the finished work of the cross.

Prophetic Declarations

Pak, thank You for separating night from day! Truly artistic You are. Pak Lord, You told Job to command the morning to favour him. You have motioned me to decree and declare a thing, and it shall establish (Job 22:28 KJV); hence I speak to the realms of the spirit and the physical with expectations that things will begin to change immediately:

I command the morning to brighten my days as it illuminates.

I command an increase as the strength of the sun increases throughout the day.

As my morning and day increases, they should overflow into the week, month and year.

I place my Angels strategically in areas (say these areas) of my life and in every country to whisper my name in people's ear with influence to look me up and favour me.

I receive grace to love all men.

I receive grace to be intentional about my spiritual growth and capacity.

I receive grace over the limitation of my senses.

I receive grace to build a good character and lifestyle.

I receive grace to resist pride and competition.

I receive grace to be accountable for my destiny.

I command doors of delay to be open to me in the name of Jesus.

Every academic bondage and mental blockage, I command you to lose your grip right now in the name of Jesus.

Whether victimized in projects, written work, on the job or in service, I change it in the spirit and physical realm in the name of Jesus.

I call forth sevenfold restoration right now in the name of Jesus.

All my loved ones and friends who require a job, I command the door of employment to open to them right now in the name of Jesus Christ.

Every plague of death over my life and loved ones, I command it to pass over us in the name of Jesus.

I call forth the anointing that will cause me to prosper and grow in wisdom in the name of Jesus Christ.

I terminate every bloodline illness right now in the name of Jesus Christ.

I command every captivity over my family to end right now in the name of Jesus Christ.

I command the spirit husband/wife to go from my life in the name of Jesus Christ.

I command the works of my hands to multiply in the name of Jesus Christ.

I command demands on my gifts and talent in the name of Jesus Christ. Thank you, Holy Spirit.

Surviving Seasons

Athair Lord, thank You for the gift of seasons. Maker of all things. Everything has a season, a time to every purpose under heaven. There is a time to plant, a time to harvest; a time to break down, a time to be strengthened; a time to weep, a time to laugh; time to mourn, a time to party, a time to get, and a time to lose (Ecclesiastes 3:1-8 WEB).

Athair Lord, when night turns to day, so shall the season of my life change. I decree and declare that I will arise and shine right now. I am no longer a victim of the powers of darkness operating to hold me down.

Athair Lord, let my sun arise. I call forth my destiny sun, financial sun, marital sun, ministerial sun to wake up. Every good and perfect gift is from above, coming down from the Athair of the heavenly lights. He does not change like shifting shadows (James 1:17 NIV).

Athair Lord, You selected me as Your chosen vessels; a royal priesthood, a holy nation, Your special possession, that I may shower praises of Him who called me out of darkness into His marvellous light (1 Peter 2:9 ESV). Through this, I receive favour from people of influence, natural spiritual powers, an increase of impact spiritually and physically in Jesus' name. Thank you, Holy Spirit, for working with me.

Freedom From Spiritual Prisons

Padre Lord, thank You for inventions. The tools to set me free. Glorious Padre. In You, O Lord, I put my trust; let me never be ashamed: deliver me in thy righteousness. Bend down Your ear to me; deliver me speedily: be thou my strong rock, for a house of defence to save me. For You are, my pillar and my stronghold; therefore, for thy name's sake lead me, and guide me (Psalm 31:1-3 NLT).

Padre Lord, I call upon You, O Lord; Please answer me and set me in a prominent place from my jailer. I decree and declare that I am free from every spiritual prison. In whatever form I am bound, may it be a prison cell, a tree padlocked, bind with chains, locked in a bottle, buried in a hole, a doll representing me pierced with needles.

I will tread about in freedom, for I abide by Your precepts. So, if the Son set me free, I am free indeed (John 3:8 WEB) in Jesus' name. Thank you, Holy Spirit, for working with me.

Forgiveness

Itay Lord, thank You for the gift of reconciliation. Precious, You are. With all my heart, I genuinely want to forgive everyone who has done me wrong. I still feel hurt every time I remember what took place. The pain took on a life of its own without being fed.

Itay Lord, I know Your words. It tells me to be kind and compassionate to another, forgive each other, just as Christ Jesus forgave me (Ephesians 4:32 NIV). If I forgive men their trespasses, my heavenly Itay will also forgive me: But if I choose not to forgive men their trespasses, neither will my Itay forgive my trespasses (Matthew 6:14-15 NLT).

Itay Lord, If I am called by your name, humble myself, pray, seek Your face, and turn from my wicked ways, You will hear from heaven and forgive me of my sins and heal my land (2 Chronicles 7:14 KJV). Please extend healing to my mind and spirit, Itay. I surrender my mind will and emotions to You, do Your will in me, and rid me of these feelings I struggle to resolve in Jesus' name. Thank you, Holy Spirit, for working with me.

Influence And Affluence

Abbu Lord, thank You for grace and mercies. Mighty, victorious, ever knowing, my present help You are. A mustard seed represents the kingdom of heaven. It is the least among all seeds: but when it is grown, it is the greatest among aromatic plants and becomes a tree so that the birds of the air come and lodge in its branches (Matthew 13:32 ESV).

Abbu Lord, please bless me indeed, enlarge my coast, and let Your hands glide me to influence and affluence. Abbu please remove the veil that is covering me from being seen. Just as yeast is not diluted or manipulated by other ingredients, so shall my life be.

Abbu Lord, in the worst moments and situations, this is when I will shine. Yeast is an agent of change. It holds things together, so shall I help nations through my influence and affluence in the name of Jesus. Because God and man favour me. Everyone around me will thrive just as Lot did by being around Abraham in Jesus name. Thank you, Holy Spirit.

Facing Natural Disaster

Vader Lord, thank You for providing a way out of disasters. Compassionate are You. Be lenient to me, O God, be compassionate to me, for in You my soul takes asylum; in the shadow of Your wings, I will take refuge, till the storms of destruction pass by (Psalm 57:1 ESV). Your words of comfort, I will not have anxiety over unexpected disaster or destruction that surpasses the wicked (Proverbs 3:25 NLT). The Lord is standing by my side and keep my foot from being snared. God, You're my refuge and strength, an ever-present help in trouble. Therefore, I will not fear, though the earth gives way and the mountains fall into the heart of the sea (Psalm 43:1-2 NKJV). I will not panic. I will say of the Lord, You are my sanctuary and fortification, my place of safety; You are my God, and I trust You (Psalm 91:2 NIV).

Vader Lord, I know that if my earthly home is destroyed, I have a building from You, one not made with mortal hands, eternal in the heavens (2 Corinthians 5:1 NLT). No matter what disaster occurs, You will be with me; Should the rivers and sea overflow, they will not sweep over me. When I pass through the fire, I will not burn; the flames will not set me ablaze. In times of misfortune, You will protect me (Isaiah 43:2 KJV). You will hide me. You will keep me safe on top of a mighty rock. The Lord is good, a shelter in times of trouble. He cares for those who have confidence in Him.

Vader lord, You're mightier than the thunder of the great waters, more powerful than the breakers of the sea called hurricane and tsunamis—the Lord on high is mighty. The rain fell, and floods came, the winds blew and beat on my house, but it did not fall because it's founded on the rock called Jesus Christ. I am secure amid natural disasters in Jesus' name. Thank you, Holy Spirit, for being there in times of trouble.

Positive Thinking

Tay Lord, thank You for the gift of restoration. Awesome wonder. I will do everything without murmurings and disputings: That which goes into the mouth does not taint a man, but that which comes out of the mouth, this defiles a man (Matthew 15:11 ESV). Either make the tree upright, and its fruits good, or else make the tree corrupt and its fruits evil. For the tree is recognized by its fruits (Matthew 12:33 NIV). How can I speak negatively and expect good things? A fool's mouth is his complete destruction, and his lips are the snare of his soul (Proverbs 18:7 KJV). Death and life located in the tongue's power, and those who love it will eat its fruits (Proverbs 18:21 WEB). For out of the fullness of the heart, the mouth speaks. I can do everything because Christ strengthens me.

Tay Lord, I will preserve my life by tailoring the way I think and speak. My words have power that derives from my thoughts. I will not conform to this world's pattern but transformed by renewing my mind (Romans 12:2 NIV). I have the mind of Christ, which is positive thinking in Jesus' name. Thank you, Holy Spirit.

Purging Bloodline

Otac Lord, thank You for Your shed blood on the cross, loving Otac. Cleanse me with hyssop, and I will be clean; wash me, and I will be whiter than snow (Psalms 51:7 NIV). Otac atoning sacrifice for my sins, not only for mine but also for the sins of all humanity. You will cleanse my blood, for that which has not purified must be edited: for Jehovah lives in Zion (Joel 2:21 ASV).

Otac Lord, I lay at the altar the sins of my forefathers. I confess that my bloodline is corrupt. It is entangled with blood sacrifices, covenants made to other gods, sexual covenants, financial covenants, the life, and destinies of people destroyed. I receive a spiritual blood transfusion to purge my bloodline in the name of Jesus. Thank you, Holy Spirit, for carrying out this transfusion in my family of origin.

Spirit Of Control And Manipulation

Abeoji Lord, thank You for making a way of escape for us from the spirit of Jezebel. You genuinely care for us. The essence of Jezebel has resurfaced and trying to destroy my (example- home, marriage, ministry, business, reputation, friendship, children, church etc.) through the works of the flesh and manifesting through immorality, idolatry, strife, pride, hatred, and bitterness (Galatians 5:19 ASV). My hope is in You Abeoji.

I call forth the spirit, power and might that overthrow Jezebel when Jehu ordered her eunuchs to throw her through the window. Abeoji, my mighty warrior whose sword is in His mouth, destroyed the works of Jezebel; You saved Your people. I call upon the God of assertiveness to slay this false prophetess and end her operation in my (repeat the area attacked) in Jesus' name. Thank you, Holy Spirit, for standing firm to the end of this battle.

Defeating Principalities And Powers

Apa Lord, thank You for shed blood at the cross. You are making a way of escape for us. You are fantastic, glorious, and supreme. Apa, come and manifest Yourself in this battle. Manifest Your great power, oh Lord.

The ground is the Lord's, and the fulness thereof; the world, and they that dwell therein. He founded it upon the seas and formed it upon the floods. Who shall ascend into the hill of the Lord? or who shall stand in his holy place? He that has unsoiled hands and a clean heart, who have not lifted his soul unto vanity, nor sworn deceitfully (Psalms 24:1-4 ESV).

So, principalities and powers, you have no right to occupy this territory. I stand before you to cast you out. It is not by my capacity but by the blood of my Lord and saviour, Jesus Christ. I decree and declare I can do everything because Christ has strengthened me.

I stand on the authority given to me by the Lord Jesus Christ. I will dislodge you. It has been said, strangers shall submit to me as soon as they hear me, they shall be obedient to me. All strangers shall disappear and become afraid in their closed places (Psalms 18:44-45 KJV). Principalities and powers leave (call the name of the place they should leave)-you are strangers in this land. I command you to get out of (repeat the area) in Jesus' name. Thank You, Jesus, thank You, Jesus. Every tree that my Apa has not planted shall be pulled out from the root (Matthew 15:13 ESV). Spirit of (murder, robbery, prostitution, low self-esteem, unemployment, teenage pregnancy, drought, victimization, mass sickness, specific illness, discord, drug, and alcohol abuse) leave this territory now in Jesus' name. Thank you, Holy Spirit, for being part of the battle over this territory.

Overcome Pride And Deceit

Bap Lord, thank You for the gift of life through salvation. My battle axe and club. On that day, the Lord with his painful, dreadful, and mighty sword shall punish Leviathan, the sharp serpent, even Leviathan that crooked serpent, and he shall slay the dragon that is in the sea (Isaiah 27:1 NIV).

Leviathan, king in the marine kingdom, which governs pride and deceit, you have caused my eyes to haughty looking down on others and seeing myself more significant than I am.

Bap Lord, oh have the mighty fallen. You have crippled the moving of the Holy Spirit in my life. You are a spirit that wrecks everything in your path. You're responsible for the ruin of mighty men of God, marriages, homes, ministries, and destinies. Leviathan, your operations are like Jezebel, and the Lord God solid and robust dealt with her, so shall He do with you.

Bap Lord, You will take Your sharp, great, and mighty sword and bring judgment on Leviathan. The Lord, will crush you like an Ant and dismantle your operations in my life. Lord, smash the heads of Leviathan; and feed them to the beings of the desert. Leviathan your downfall will mend the relationship between my Lord and me. I will be restored in the name of Jesus Christ. Thank you, Holy Spirit.

Immigration Issues

My Padre, my Padre, thank You for settling the matter of immigration. There is no doubt that You are for immigrants-when You commanded the Israelites not to mistreat hired help even if they are immigrants. The immigrants are poor and in need (Exodus 22:21-22 NKJV). Padre, You are the most thoughtful and amazing Padre there is. Your earthly parents had to immigrate before You were born and shortly after Your birth. Great are You, Padre.

Padre Lord, I didn't enter (say the name of the country you're in) through the back door. I never paid anyone to commit fraud or falsified documents on my behalf. Neither did I travel in a name other than my own.

I am here in (say the name of the country you're in) struggling to settle. You told Abraham to move from where he was so You could indeed bless him. Abraham obeyed, and You multiplied him.

When we immigrate, it should be for Your glory, an opportunity to lift Your banner high. I desire that other individual will come to know that You're no respecter of anyone. What You do for one person You can and will do for anyone who submits their life to You.

It was Your permissive will that took Joseph to Egypt. People knew of Your mighty works through the gifts in him. He saved the lives of his family and many others because Your permissive will took him to another country to dwell. It is that same permissive will that brought me here. Please have mercy and grant me favour with (say the name of the country you're in) immigration Services in the name above every name: Jesus Christ. Thank you, Holy Spirit, for being with me throughout this process; I know you will continue to guide me to the end.

Grace To Be Genuine

Abba Lord, thank You for Your administration in my life. You are truly outstanding. Abba, sometimes I serve but only to be recognized or praised. I have an inner hunger to be seen. I am no better than the disciples. When You called, they quickly followed You. Peter was married, and without thought, he left everything to follow You.

As time went by, the secrets of their hearts began to unfold-they were with You for what they could gain, power and influence. Abba, help me to become a genuine servant, as the disciples did when they experienced You in the name of Jesus Christ. Thank you, Holy Spirit, for your consistent tugging at my heart to change.

Dry Bones Live

Aita Lord, the giver of life, I thank You. Praise be to You for Your notable works in the lives of humanity. Aita, my trust is in You only. When man fails, You will never forget me. Lord, You told Ezekiel to prophesy to the dry bones in the valley, and he did according to Your will. They were renewed, completely restored.

Aita, therefore by faith, I prophesy to the dry bones in my life. Dry bones of marital issues, dry bones of failure in ministry, connections, influence, dormant gifts, financial barrenness, you will live-I call forth breath and sinew upon you now in the name of Jesus Christ. Thank you, Holy Spirit, for the expressed will of God.

Restitution

Bap Lord, thank You for being merciful unto me. You are fantastic, Bap. I am required to make restitution base on Your laws Bap. This is difficult for me to carry. It was done in secret, and no one knows of it. Please help me. The stress of just thinking about it is too much for me. Mercy Lord, teach me how to carry out this without it becoming a regretful situation.

Bap, the heart of men, is in Your hands. Please touch their hearts. Give them a forgiving heart. Please remove shame from me as I seek to be in oneness with You in the name above every other name, Jesus Christ. Thank you, Holy Spirit.

My Brothers' Keeper

Far Lord, thank You for not holding my faults against me continually but have made provision for them to be blotted out. Life-giver, I worship You. Sibling rivalry is an age-old thing beginning with Cain and Abel. We have also seen it in the story of Joseph.

Far Lord, sibling rivalry is present in my family from generation to generation. It has been there. If I cannot love my siblings that I can see, I don't love You whom I cannot see. I want to be at peace with everyone. If I am angry with my sibling, I will be judged for this. It seems like a small matter, but before You, Lord, it is grand. Please, Lord, help us love each other genuinely so that it will be right between You and me in the name of Jesus Christ. Thank you, Holy Spirit, for being an advocate in the situation.

Remembrance

Buwa Lord, thank You for being a rewarder. Supreme, every lasting Buwa. Buwa, You know and remember everything I have done. Still, You told me to remind You of things I did to be rewarded. King Hezekiah received a word from You about his pending death. He went before You and pleaded his case. He brought evidence to support his claim before You.

Buwa Lord, I am before You to plead my case. I have brought with me evidence to support my claim before You as requested. I have worshipped only You. I have supported Your work financially and through service. I have served in these capacities (say the areas you worked in for God) without the hope of being rewarded. The situation on the ground requires Your urgent intervention. I ask that You review the case set before You and grant me a favour with men in the name more excellent than every other name, Jesus Christ, my advocate. Thank you, Holy Spirit, for being my comforter in a time when I needed you.

Binding The Strong Man

Abeoji Lord, thank You for making a way to elude the devil. The proven stronger man. The operations of Satan are very evident in my life. The door was open, and he entered. Now there is chaos in my family. Abeoji, You are the most potent one. I call on You because it is only through using Your authority will Satan back off.

Abeoji, if I am to take plunder and carry away the captives in my family, I will first need bind the strongman operating in my lineage. Abeoji, not on my strength, oh Lord, but Yours. Satan has stolen destinies, investments, works of our hands, opportunities, and marriages. Let the thief be disarmed, disinherited, disposed of every he took from us in Jesus' name. Strongman assigned to my lineage on my mother and father side I bind you in the name of Jesus. Strong man, your activities have been crippled through the might of Jesus' name. The Lord rebukes your operation over the next generations to come too. Your operation has expired collectively and individually in my lineage. Thank you, Holy Spirit.

Home Ownership

Otosan Lord, thank You for providing for the birds of the air because the same provision is there for me too. The master builder. Competent Architect. I am a resident of the earth; therefore, I must own part of it. I will possess possessions. I will own houses and lands. While I am here, I will comfortably acquire assets.

Otosan, come and take Your place at my house. You're welcome in every room. There is no boundary to where You can occupy. May the spirit of ownership come on everyone that enters one of my houses. Let Your peace reign now and always in these houses in the name above every other name Jesus Christ. Thank you, Holy Spirit.

Calling Forth Mantles And Graces

Vader Lord, thank You for showing us what mantles and graces can do for us and others. The giver of good things. Please, Vader, restore time in my life. Right throughout the Bible, I have seen mantles and graces operating in the lives of individuals, which caused them to do extraordinary things. Vader, I am not satisfied with being an ordinary person. I desire to be a significant person working with the real power of He who created all things. The word tells me anything I ask for in the name of Your only Son will be granted unto me.

I call forth the mantle and grace of my Lord Jesus Christ to cast out demons, raise the dead, command permanent healing, cause things to multiply in the name of Jesus Christ.

I call forth the mantle and grace of Elijah, passed down to Elisha, which wasn't passed down to anyone else to rest on me right now in the name of Jesus Christ.

I call forth the mantles and graces of all Old Testament Prophets to rest on me instantly in the name of Jesus Christ.

I call forth the mantle and grace of David, Joshua and Deborah for strategic battle plan and execution to rest on me right now in the name of Jesus Christ.

I call forth the mantle and graces of Joseph and Daniel to interpret dreams and political influence to rest on me right now in the name of Jesus Christ.

I call forth the mantle and grace on Esther to be loved and favour by everyone who came across her to rest on me right now in the name of Jesus Christ.

I call forth the mantle and graces of the eleven apostles and Paul to know, understand, analyse, interpret scriptures, teach, and preach the word of God in the name of Jesus Christ.

Holy Spirit, please keep me in line constantly. I don't ever want to misuse these mantles and graces. I desire to be humble and direct all glory to Jesus Christ for the works in peoples' lives.

Right DNA

Apu Lord, thank You for shed blood on the cross. I praise You for the mystery of blood. Apu, I desire a blood transfusion. I want to have suitable DNA blended and flowing in my blood.

The sons of Sceva did not have the suitable DNA and attempted to cast out evil spirits, and they were criticized, embarrassed because the kingdom of darkness didn't recognize the blood in them. The demons acknowledged knowing Jesus Christ and can identify Paul. Apu Lord, let my life come in alignment with Your ordinances, for the transfusion to take place in the name of Jesus Christ. Thank you, Holy Spirit, for being my teacher.

Break The Curse Of Hand To Mouth

Faoir Lord, thank You for serving the poor when You were here. I praise You for being self-giving. The poor will always exist. Withstanding does not mean that I should accept living in dire poverty. The resources that come in can only do a little. I reject this way of life.

Faoir Lord, I bind the spirit of hand to mouth fostered by the injustice which needs to shut its mouth. I decree and declare I will eat the good of the land. Wealth and riches are stored in my house. My barns are full of wheat and other provisions. I have various animals at my disposal. The bank opened an account for me without me going there. My influence is excellent. My name represents multiple currencies in the name of Jesus Christ. Thank you, Holy Spirit.

Abortion

Baaba Lord, thank You for being the one and only giver of life. I marvel at Your wonderous work. You are against taking the life of the innocent and helpless. I have killed my unborn child/children. Honestly, I would do it again, considering being in the same situation.

Baaba, by the standard of Your word, the blood of the unborn is seeking vengeance. I humbly ask for Your forgiveness and that the spirit of my child/children will find rest in You. Please repair the parts of my nature that broken from the abortion(s) I have done in the name of Jesus Christ. Thank you, Holy Spirit, for never abandoning me during my selfish moment(s).

Unnatural Desires

Pai Lord, thank You for making me unique. You are awesome. I am attracted to the same sex. Your word is not clear on the matter. No scripture speaks to what I am feeling. You created everything, male, and female. I appreciate that. The account of Sodom and Gomorrah being destroyed for their many sins. This account is still not clear. It specifically said Lot offered his daughter because they want to rape the angels. Pai, the keyword is rape.

Pai Lord, what could cause me to have these feelings? Lord, please show me myself in the name of Jesus Christ. Thank you, Holy Spirit, for assisting me, supreme Pai, in the works of my life.

Frontline Enemy

Ama Lord, thank You for calling and choosing humankind to serve You on the battlefield. The greatest, mightiest, most robust warrior. I have transgressed against You and my family. I have neglected my first ministry, my family.

Ama lord, I go about serving others and have neglected to serve my own family. I have been a counsellor to other people's children, and my children don't receive the same time from me. I have not made time to speak with them when they requested it or have intentional conversations with them. The enemy left the battlefield and went to my family, as in the Sisera battle. My children have been attacked, and my marriage is threatened.

Ama Lord, please forgive me for neglecting my first ministry, my own family. Without the corporation of my husband/wife, I cannot have a triumphant ministry. Please have mercy on me and heal the heart of my family and destroyed the enemy as the wife of the Soldier did in the name of Jesus Christ. Thank you, Holy Spirit, for holding me accountable to my family.

Conspiracies

Itay Lord, thank You, for grace and mercies. You are the most genuine one. Deceptive people surround me. Itay, we have seen in the word where David's counsellor Ahithophel joined Absalom to unseat David. When David found out, he asked God to let Ahithophel work be of no importance. God fought for David; all his enemies died.

Itay lord, let my conspirators' counsel become imprudent. Let confusion be amongst them. Overturn every evil thought towards me. Overturn every wish of death in my life. Break the snare for divine escape. Let my enemies be arrested, tried, found guilty, and sentenced to death in the realms of the spirit in the name of Jesus Christ. Thank you, Holy Spirit.

Love

Makuakāne Lord, thank You for the gift of Love. I bless Your name. Showing my love for you, I have kept your commandments. Lord, this is difficult. To love, in general, takes a lot to do. But, Makuakāne, I will try by your grace.

Makuakāne Lord, You gave us a new commandment to love one another: just as You have loved us). Through this, all people will know that we are Your believers if we show love for one another. Otherwise, anyone who does not love does not know You because You are love (John 13:34-36 NIV).

Makuakāne Lord, love is patient and kind; love does not envy or boast; it is not arrogant or rude. It does not insist on its ways; it is not irritable or resentful; it does not rejoice at wrongdoing but celebrates the truth. Love can bear all things, believes all things, hopes all things, endures all things. Love never ends (1 Corinthians 13: 4-8 NLT).

Makuakāne Lord, I need your grace and mercy to love. Please help me as I try daily to love all men in Jesus' name. Thank you, Holy Spirit, for the work you will do for me.

Scripture Sources

Bible Gateway: https://www.biblegateway.com
Bible Hub: https://www.biblehub.com

Bible Versions

Amplified (AMP)
King James Version (KJV)
New Living Translation (NLT)
New King James Version (NKJV)
New International Version (NIV)

Number of Text Used

Two Hundred and One

CPSIA information can be obtained
at www.ICGtesting.com
Printed in the USA
LVHW071648140821
695327LV00023B/2151